INTRODUCTION

Coal has been mined all over the world, from the most ancient of days. Whenever, wherever, it has been the same dirty and dangerous task; deep underground digging coal to provide warmth, steam, electricity.

This tale is an old one, told by people late in years, remembering mining life in the early 1900's.

It is a tale told as if by one person, though many have contributed to its telling. Many have lived through similar times but all are very old and soon these days will be beyond living memory.

That simply is the purpose of this story : to record memories of mining life in the early 1900's.

KEVIN THOMPSON
August 1991

The Colliers Tale

One fine summer morning - I can remember it now - my dad took off for a walk up in the woods. He always took the dog with him. They used to range for miles together.

When he came home, we knew something was wrong.
He said he'd got to report to the colliery office first thing Monday morning. The dog had caught a rabbit up in the woods, and the woods belonged to the colliery. Worst of all, the game keeper had seen it happen, and accused him of poaching.

Monday morning, the choice was simple,

> *"Have the dog put down or loose your job."*
> *"I'll not have the dog put down."* my dad said,
> *"he's done nothing wrong."*

He got another job the same day at another pit. But it meant he had to walk eleven miles there, and eleven miles back. Every day.

My mum would sometimes say,

> *"Your dad's late, you had better go look for him."*

So, I would set off over the fields. Before long I'd find him, asleep in a hedgerow Overcome by fatigue he was just too tired to carry on. Anyway, I'd wake him and he would stumble home in a trance.
Too tired to wash, my mum would have to scrub off his pit black and take his moleskins to repair for the next day.

Then he'd fall asleep again, exhausted.

I started working down the pit when I was fourteen ... my last resort at getting a job. Me and me dad, we had tried everything. But, there was nothing. The pit was the only option, and that was that.

Anyway, next thing I knew, it was Monday morning, six o'clock, I was waiting to go down. The 'Onsetter' spotted me getting in the cage and as he shut the gate, he waved to the engine driver - then the engine driver knew he'd got a fresh chap on the cage.

Down we went, fast into the dark. I grabbed the chap next to me, I was that frightened. Then, about half way down,
I thought we were going back up again,
he'd put the brakes on.

Every fresh faced chap, first time down, 'Onsetter' would wave to the engine driver and down you'd go. Like a stone.

Then, you'd a three-quarter of an hour walk just to get to your district, and your shift didn't start 'til you got there. It was terrible.

Anyway, after a few weeks dodging about, first with one pony driver and then another, I did six months battery carrying and then went pony driving.

By lad, it was hot, we used to wear 'nics', short 'nics',
it was that hot.

They came off the moors the ponies did. Wild ponies from the Black Mountains. One of my jobs was breaking them in. You used to put the tackle on them and at first they didn't know whether to push or pull; sometimes I'd have to get behind the wagons and shove them before they'd start drawing.

There were two stables at the pit, and about seventy ponies all together. There were some smashing ponies - greys, blacks, whites, all colours. All friends and all faithful ... 'Sangster', 'Pony Ben', 'Turpin' ...

They could get about in the dark you know. I'd sit on the shaft-iron with my light shining but 'Toby' didn't bother if it was lit or not. If he came to a door he'd nuzzle it with his nose and shove it open. Sometimes he'd stop and start, then you knew something was the matter - you was ever mindful of your pony.
Then, you would hear creaking, creaking. You would back him down and then, there would be a roof fall.

A pit pony saved many a mans life through that.

Every morning I'd take 'Toby' a bag of grass, a little sandbag full of new mown grass. As soon as I went in the stable he could smell it ... and he'd start to whinny. He'd have a bag of corn everyday - he'd stop at his own will at his corn tub and have a mouthful and then off he'd go, with me sitting on the shaft iron.

At that time, if a pony got as he couldn't do any work, he'd be sold. He'd go up and be sold for perhaps two pounds and be used for pulling coal carts. Anyway, one chap was seen whacking his pony - he could not draw his load up the hill. He was spotted by the agents son. He went to the pit office and wanted to know the chaps name.

"Don't let him have any more coal, No more."

he said.

That finished him.

Then, the agents son went to the stable bailiff and said,

"In future, all ponies coming out of the pit will be shot. I'm not going to have them sold for two pounds and then be worked to death."

And that was that.

When the ponies were too old and tired to work anymore, they took them up and shot them.

Then, one day, the seam broke out with gas, just up by where we were working. It just used to loom up, a big cloud as thick as your body. Like blue smoke. I'll never forget. And then, the men loomed up out of it. The deputy was shouting.

> *"Get the men out!*
> *Get the ponies out!"*

The men were hysterical.
They'd got the gas down them.

They were tumbling and stumbling about and when they hit the clear air they were worse. My brother got it bad; he was the last out, trying to save his old pony 'Taff'.

He kept trying to lift him up, struggling with him.

Me and the stall men carried old 'Taff' and my brother into the clean air. Down they went. My brother popped right out. We thought he was going to die, he kept stiffening out. Anyway, he slept it off but he was never right since. It finished his lungs off and he never worked down the pit again.

It finished that seam off as well and my wages fell from sixteen shillings a day to six and eight pence.

That was that.

I was eighteen.

It took 'til I was twenty-one to alter things. I asked the manager for my own stall.
The manager said

"You're a bit young to be a charge man."

I said,

"Well, I know the job, I want you to give me a chance.
I want some money to get married on.
I've got my own tools. I've a stand, drills, worm and handle, pick and shovel."

"Well, start Wednesday." he said.

This was Friday evening.

But, Monday came first. It was cold and damp.
The 'Onsetter' hurried us onto the cage. It was ten-to-seven and by seven he was expected to be bringing up coal.

About half way down, panic gripped us. We were going fast. Much to fast.

"We're going to crash!" I shouted.

Plummeting down we went. I dropped my lamp and jumped to catch the bars of the cage roof. At the same time the cage smashed into the pit bottom, tearing through the sump boards and coming to rest half submerged in cold, stagnant water. From the racket of the crash an eerie silence settled over the mangled beams, bars, and men. I was seized with a choking sensation.

I felt dazed and very sick.

One chap had gone clean through the cage bottom, his body nearly submerged in the sump water.

"Lift me up a bit Jesse." he called to his mate.

Jesse's movements caused great pain to someone. Out of the blackness I heard a cry of great distress. Jesse raised the man a bit but he fell back crying. His back was broken. Again, silence. Cold and shocked, one by one we passed out. By lad, we'd had it.

Later, we found out more about it. They hadn't a clue how to rescue us. The only other way down the pit was via the 'up-going' shaft and that was out of action, the 'up-going' cage had smashed into the 'headstocks'. All they could do was free the 'up-going' cage, repair it, then lower it; and that took ages.

It took from seven 'til a quarter to two to get us out.

They had decided that we would not survive the usual journey to hospital in the pony drawn tub, so they arranged for a train to be brought to the siding.

Compared to the others I was alright. I had dislocated both knees and gashed my head. Jesse had died, his back broken. A young lad, Amos, he had to have his leg amputated it was that badly broken. His dad also had to have his leg amputated but he died shortly after the operation. Shock, I suppose. Everyone of the other men had complicated compound fractures of the legs.

People said it was lucky that the accident had happened on a Monday morning. As no one had worked on Sunday night, no one was in the 'up-going' cage - had there been, they would have suffered instant death when the cage rammed the 'headstocks'.

Anyway, the coroner at the inquest said the engine man was to blame. He knew his brakes were faulty and that he'd dropped the cage too fast in his rush to get the men down. The hapless engine driver wished he was dead. He had reported the faulty brake twice and nothing had been done and he was in trouble if he wasn't bringing up coal by seven. I can't remember what became of him, but he never came near the pit again.

"Start Wednesday." the manager had said.

Some chance.

I did start back soon after though - with my own stall - but it hadn't been easy. Our pit didn't have insurance cover, so if you were injured, the pit had to pay your wages. I had to start back before I was anything like ready - but they said I was ready, so it was start back or no money.

So, that was that.

Getting The Coal

Anyway, from the pit bottom ran a big tunnel called the main haulage. This served as the main road to the district you were working. From the main haulage, cross gates ran across the coal face from which the stall roads fanned out creating the separate working compartments, or stalls.

Usually, the main haulage would be what you would call 'man high' to allow for upright walking, but not always. Certainly, the roadways off the main haulage were no more than 'pony high' so you had to crouch when you went down those. The roads down to your stall might only be as high as the coal seam, perhaps only three or four foot. Not even your pony could get down them, so you had to push the tubs to the pony. Many a pony would chafe his back or cut his head if he was not mindful of his whereabouts.

There were two ways of getting the coal, the large butty system and the small butty system.

The large butty system meant around ten butty's or contractors - sharing all the money and then paying the men who had produced it. This was not very popular as the men never knew how much the butty's had been given in the first place.

With the small butty system the coal face was divided into stalls, each stall being worked by a team of three men, 'fillers' and pony drivers. The headman in the stall would be paid for the coal his stall produced. He would then divide the money between them.

Once the stall road had been tunnelled out and the roof supported by wooden props, the coal could be got.

The 'holer' would drive steel wedges into the bottom of the coal face to chip off blocks of coal, creating a ridge underneath. This was very hard work and very dangerous too, lying on your side, chipping out coal. You had to knock in 'sprags' as well, to prevent the ridge roof falling on top of you.

In my dads day, just before I started down the pit, the stall men used to get all the coal using hammer and wedges. The coal was broken in to pieces about two and a half foot long and was loaded edgeways on flat bottomed tubs with sides about 6" deep. When the tubs were loaded, bands of iron called 'garlands' were fastened round to hold the coal firm on its rough ride to the haulage.

But then, 'black powder' was introduced. This meant smaller coal could be produced and production increased. High sided tubs replaced the low ones and instead of using hammer and wedges, the face men drilled holes to put dynamite in and blow the coal out.

The 'powder' was dangerous. I'll tell you what I can remember as plain as if it was yesterday.

They used to store the explosive in a powder shed, no bigger than a pigeon loft.

Well, one Friday dinner, it blew up!!
The whole town thought a bomb had gone off!!

Old Jack that was in there, they never found a particle of him, or his pony. They were blown to smithereens!!

Black powder, as well as producing smaller coal, created 'slack' for which there was no demand. Keeping the 'slack' out of the tubs created problems for the management. They tried many ways to beat the 'slackers' as they called the men who were caught.

One of the methods of beating the 'slackers' was to employ a 'slack bobby', who had to be very thick skinned as they received a lot of abuse. They moved from stall to stall, generally without a light, to try and catch the stall men filling the tubs with shovels instead of large 'tinned' forks, which allowed anything less than two inches to fall through. Anyone they caught would lose time off work.

As the coal was hacked and blown out and loaded onto tubs, props were hammered in to support the roof. The space the coal had been taken from was called the 'gob hole'. Serious fires could start if shoddy stall men threw 'slack' or damaged props into them. A good stall man made sure nothing was in the 'gob hole', just the props and stone packing for the roof.

Well anyway, that's how it was.

Dirty and dangerous.

But we all stood together.

En Bloc.

We had to.

Hard Times for Everyone

How could I go on strike? I'd only been married a while and my wife was expecting her first baby. We'd not got a penny saved - you never had a penny to save.

At the beginning of the strike you could go into work but you needed a police escort. My wife was having a baby, we'd got no baby clothes, no nothing, so I said I was going in.

The police came and escorted me and three others through the town. The men were all there and they booed us as we walked through and shouted,

"Blackleg! Blackleg!"

Some spat at us.

We had the same treatment coming home.

"I can't go through that again," I said, *"not against all my mates."*

We went on the means test and got five shillings or something a week.

Well, that was no good to me.

We needed two pounds and ten shillings for the midwife, to order the doctor was three pounds. You had to pay the doctor in advance, whether you called him out or not. Going to hospital was just too expensive.

We were desperate.

We were hungry that year. There were plenty of dinner times, but there weren't many dinners. Some of my mates, their children went down to the chapel to the soup kitchen, but when they found out their dads were digging for coal on the common, they stopped them.

They were hard times for the kids. You'd see them scrattin' around on the tip, looking for empty bottles to take back to the pub at a penny a time, or jam jars for ha'penny.

They'd run round doing all these errands to get a penny to take the hunger off, but the running around would make them hungrier.

They couldn't win!

I don't know who thought of it, but a lot of us ended up digging for coal in the woods, and on the common. Some even dug shafts in their back gardens! "Feddin'" we called it, after the union. We'd dig out a shaft, twenty or thirty feet deep and get the coal out at a bucket a time and stack it at the top. We'd sink two shafts so we could join them up to help the air get round. We also paid a lad to 'watch out' that no one pinched the coal; no one did but they might have done !

They'd come from the potteries in steam wagons and buy the coal for cash, two pounds a ton. Some of the miners would buy gallon bottles of beer with the money.

One night they got so drunk some fell down the shafts!

I told my dad - he said,

> *"The beer isn't that good,*
> *its what they wash the aprons in!"*

I was up in the woods every day, morning 'til night. I'd go home, at night worn right out, we had to dig down thirty foot before we reached coal. I was just thinking all the time about the baby and getting the money, but the coal was there and by gum, I was going to get it out.

One night I went home and put seven pounds in her lap ! She thought she was a millionaire.

Two days later I got another three pounds. All the bills were covered. Just after that the baby came, my dad gave us a pound. He'd been fighting a compensation claim for nystagmus - 'pit blindness' - and he'd won his case. He only won a few pounds but it helped them out.

If I hadn't gone feddin', I don't know what would have become of us.

During the strike my brother heard they were working in Nottingham, so he went over there. He found out that if he wanted a stall, he would have to leave the union.

The under manager said,

> *"Until you sign the Spencers agreement, no job. Leave your union."*

So he came back and went feddin' again but the colliery stopped them digging and they brought the police in.

He ended up in prison for defying the ban.

COAL MINING IN A GARDEN AT NEWHALL BURTON ON TRENT

Things weren't a lot better after the strike. We went back, but only on a three day week. Some days you would be only three hours into your shift and they'd shout,

"Lillycock, all out!!"

That meant the end of your shift because you'd produced all the coal they needed, and because you'd been into work, you couldn't sign on the dole.

You could sign on in August in holiday week though, because you didn't get any pay at all then.

To try and make ends meet me and my pal used to set snares up in the fields for rabbits. About six or seven in the evening we would go and find the runs; you could tell by the marks where to set your snares.
We'd go back in the morning about four or five o'clock, and then take them and sell them.
Sixpence each.
The fellow used to sell them for nine pence, gutted and skinned. I never got caught, but I was ever mindful of what happened to my dad, all those years before.

If you got caught, you were in trouble.

BAGWORTH
COLLIERY
1990 J.H.Reid
MAYNARD ARMS

Pig Sticking!

Nearly everyone had pigs.
They used to come and kill the pigs in the back yard. A chap used to come, the 'pig sticker' we used to call him; and we had to help. Once, he'd just stuck a pig and it got away. It ran round and round the garden 'til it dropped!!

There was only the squeal wasted on a pig.

I used to catch the blood in a big tin. That was for black pudding. They used to let the pig hang for a day or two and then the man would come back again, cut it down the middle and cut its head off. We'd make brawn with that. They used to get a brick of salt and rub it into the meat to cure it, and then it would be hung in the kitchen.

Sometimes you could cut a slice of ham and eat it cold, but best of all was grilled over the range.

Neighbours that hadn't got pigs, used to bring their scraps and put them in the swill tubs to be boiled for the pigs. When you killed the pigs you would give them some brawn or black pudding in exchange. Every Sunday morning, folk would go and look at each others pigs to see how they were coming along!

They were hard times, hard times for everybody.

Some Important Dates

1842 Coal Mines Act
This made it illegal for mine owners to employ women or boys under ten to work underground.

1889 The Miners Federation of Great Britain was formed.
This was the first real national trade union. By 1890 its membership was 250,000.

1897 The Work men's Compensation Act.
This promised money to next of kin in the event of death or injury in an accident at work. Some miners had to sign forms exempting them in order to get jobs.

1908 The Eight Hours Act
This limited the length of a shift underground.

1911 Miners Regulation Act
A key Health and Safety at Work Act. But mining was still dangerous.

1913 The Senghenydd Disaster
439 miners lost their lives in an underground explosion at this pit in South Wales.

1912 Minimum Wages Act
This secured a basic minimum wage for miners.

1914 War
In 1916 the government took control of the pits, returning them to their owners in 1921.

1921 The Lock Out
The pit owners locked out the workers to force pay cuts of up to 50%.

1926 "Not a penny off the pay, not a minute on the day."
3.5 million miners went on strike to prevent the pit owners from reducing pay and lengthening the working day. Despite the 1908 Act and the 1912 Act, the pit owners had their way.

1931 Unemployment in some areas was as high as 40%.
Pay for miners was averaging six shillings and ten pence a day. Such poverty led to the famous hunger marches.

1934 The Gresford Colliery Disaster
265 men and boys lost their lives in a terrible underground explosion.

Acknowledgments

This story does not pretend to be an accurate history of the social conditions of miners and their families. It is rather, an impression of life in a particular place, at a particular time.

Should then, special mention be made of individuals in a story where every effort has been made to avoid mention of specific people and specific places?

I think so, but sparingly, and with apologies to those who will see where I have changed the truth to suit the story!!

So then, thank you to
Mr. and Mrs. Bob Budworth, collier and wife;
Mr. and Mrs. Musk, collier and wife;
also to Mr. Shaw, pitman and local author.
Thanks also to the many people who gave of their time and hospitality in remembering the incidents which, together, helped to compile 'The Colliers Tale'

With many thanks to Donisthorpe, Oakthorpe and Rawdon Collieries for their kind permission to draw underground prior to closure in 1990.

Artists comments

As an artist I drew for the last time underground at Bagworth Colliery, Leicestershire and the road 32's struck me vividly. I wanted to show the modern roads as at October 1990 with the ghosts of the miners still walking down back to the cage and/or sitting down having their 'snap'.

This Colliery is now sealed up but the roads are still there,
and the the memories....

CONTENTS

"...and how quickly they pass away, these decent people, when they are old. The slightest change of circumstances and there's nothing left of them, it's all gone in a flash."

Dostoevsky.